Child-Land

Picture-Pages for the Little Ones

Oscar Pletsch, M. Rictor

Alpha Editions

This edition published in 2021

ISBN : 9789355117991

Design and Setting By
Alpha Editions
www.alphaedis.com
Email – info@alphaedis.com

As per information held with us this book is in Public Domain.
This book is a reproduction of an important historical work. Alpha Editions uses the best technology to reproduce historical work in the same manner it was first published to preserve its original nature. Any marks or number seen are left intentionally to preserve its true form.

A MUSICAL EVENING.

This is a very pleasant way of spending a winter evening, and my young friends like it much. All young folks should learn music.

THE LITTLE COOKS.

Lucy and Jane are fond of playing at cooks, and seem very busy this morning. Lucy is standing on a stool stirring something in a pot, and Jane is watching the cups on the little stove. I hope the children will not burn themselves, nor make a mess on the floor, or mama will be very cross.

THE WHEEL OFF.

Oh dear, another accident! Only yesterday the third wheel came off the lamb that little sister used to drag about the room. And now a wheel has come off the pretty chaise in which dolly rides. But do not cry, baby; we must ask papa to mend it, and then the chaise will go as well as ever.

THE BROKEN CUP.

Laura looks very grave this morning, and no wonder, for she has broken a tea-cup.

BABY AND HIS DOLL.

Baby is busy this morning with his doll. "Bruno" is watching by his side, ready to bark at any one who comes near.

THE KIND BROTHER.

Edward is a good kind brother, for, though he has his own lessons to learn, he is holding the thread for his sister Kate, whom he is very fond of, and tries to please as much as he can.

CURIOUS JOHN.

You are too impatient and curious, Master John. Far better to have waited till papa had himself shown you the pretty toys he has brought you from the fair.

FAST ASLEEP.

The sun has been up long ago, but baby is still asleep, with dolly by his side. We will not wake him, for he went to bed last night very tired. He had been out all day playing in the garden, and seemed quite glad when it was time for him to go to bed, so we will let him sleep a little longer. This will do him more good just now than being out in the hot sun.

DOLLY'S PARTY.

This is dolly's party. The two little girls have been invited to tea with her, and they have each brought their dolls with them. I hope it will be a pleasant party, though of course our two little friends must do all the talking, as Miss Dolly, though she sits there in such state, cannot speak a single word. But I dare say they can talk for her and themselves too.

DON'T BE GREEDY.

Harriet has had some apples given her, but she is so greedy she wishes to keep them all herself. She has two lying on the sofa already, and yet she does not seem willing to give the third to her little brother. I am ashamed of you, greedy girl!

THE PUMP.

Lucy is trying to pump up some water for her little sister, but she should be careful, for the water may run out suddenly and wet little Mary's dress. If this happens mama will be angry, for her dress is a very nice one indeed, and almost new.

THE LOST BALL.

Oh dear, oh dear, what shall we do,
For we have lost the ball?
The water-butt is deep, and now
We cannot play at all.

LEARNING TO WALK.

Mama is giving little Mary her first lesson in walking. She is of course rather timid, but she will learn presently, when she has got a little more confidence.

THE SICK DOLL.

The doctor has just come in to see the sick doll, and is feeling her pulse. He tells Mary not to be alarmed, for her doll is no worse, and will be quite well in a day or two if she is kept quiet. I am sure Mary will attend to this, as she is very anxious about her doll, and would be sorry to lose her.

FEEDING THE BIRDS.

Well done, well done, thoughtful Jane,
At your morning work again,
Feeding thus with grain and crumbs
Every hungry bird that comes:
Well they know you, I can see,
Or they would more timid be.

HELPING MOTHER.

Well done, Emma! Dinner is just over, and Emma is folding up the cloth, and tidying up.

WHAT'S IN THE CUPBOARD?

Mama has just caught the children prying into the cupboard. She will be angry with them, I am sure, for being so inquisitive.

ALL TO OURSELVES.

Little Emma and George have shut themselves into an up-stairs room this morning, and are pretending to be papa and mama. They have got papa's great boots on the floor, and Emma has dressed the boot-jack like a doll, and placed mama's bonnet on her head. Mama down-stairs will wonder presently what has become of her two little pets.

THE WASHING-TUB.

Our little friends are busy this morning, for dolly's washing must be done before dinner. But there are two of them, and they have got a nice large tub, so they will soon get it done. It will be well for poor dolly when her clothes are washed and ironed, for she must be very uncomfortable lying there on the floor.

"TEACH ME TO DRAW, PLEASE."

The children have come to see their uncle, the artist. They like to come and look at his pictures, and they are asking him to teach them to draw. It is a nice thing to be able to draw well.

DRESSED UP.

Little Richard has been dressing himself up in some old clothes, and has got a big walking-stick. His brother is amused, but baby does not seem to know him.

THE GROCER.

Mr. Sweet, the grocer, is serving his customers. James has just had some treacle, but he has put his finger into the jug, and is sucking it. Naughty boy!

"IT DOESN'T TICK."

Mama, my watch does not tick, as papa's does. I wish you would make it tick.

JUST THE SIZE.

Our two little friends have been out to-day with their mama, to buy some stockings for their dolls. They have just returned, and are fitting them on, and find they are just the size. The youngest of the doll family is snug in her cradle; but the doll lying on her face on the drawers, must, I fear, be very uncomfortable. They will notice it presently, I dare say.

DOLLY'S WASHING.

It is a very serious affair when the day comes round to do dolly's washing. Lines are hung up in the nursery, with a great tub to hold the wet clothes, and, after that, they are hung across the lines to dry. Our two little friends are as busy as they can be, and they must make haste, for papa would not like to find his little girls absent when he comes home.

THE INTERRUPTION.

Do not interrupt our play, brother Tom. Please go back to your lessons.

LUCY'S NEW BONNET.

That bonnet is too smart, Lucy. I fear you are too fond of dress.

THE CONCERT.

The children have got papa's music books, and are pretending to sing from them. Even dolly is stuck up against the wall, as if she were one of the singers. The dog is listening, as though he would ask what is the meaning of all this strange noise, and is barking, himself, very dismally, to add to it.

THE BROKEN DOLL.

This is a sad affair indeed. Little Jane dropped her pretty new doll on the floor while she was playing with her cousin, and now it is broken and spoiled. She is crying as if she would break her little heart over the disaster, but all her tears will not mend dolly again. But perhaps papa will buy her another, if she asks him.

THE NOSEGAY.

Little Laura has just opened the garden gate, and is hurrying off to school. She has a nosegay in her hand, which she is taking to her governess, whom she is very fond of. I dare say the governess will like her little present, for every one is fond of flowers, and still more the kindness which prompted her to bring it.

BABY BROTHER.

Our little baby brother is quite a romp. He is full of fun, and it is hard to keep him out of mischief. He kicks his boots off, pulls off his socks, and his new little woolly lamb and cart were soon torn to pieces. He plays with Bruno in a very rough way, and it is a wonder the dog bears it so patiently. This morning he has seized Tom by the hair, and seems highly pleased to have the chance of giving it a good pull.

READY FOR SCHOOL.

Mama is plaiting Ellen's hair this morning, and then she will be ready for school. Though her toys are on the floor beside her, yet she stands quite still, like a good girl.

"THERE'S A GOOD DOGGIE."

FEEDING THE FOWLS.

Baby is giving some bread-crumbs to the fowls this morning. The cock looks up as though he would say "Thank you."

BEING WASHED.

Baby is screaming because he does not like to be washed. This is very naughty.

THE ROPERY.

Poor little James has come down to the ropery, to see the men make string. He has got a great ball of string to fly his kite with.

THE BROKEN WATERING-POT.

Susan is very sad this evening, for she has broken her little watering-pot, and so she does not know how to water her flowers.

SHOEING THE HORSE.

Let him have a good shoe, please, Mr. Farrier, and take care you don't hurt him, for he is a noble fellow.

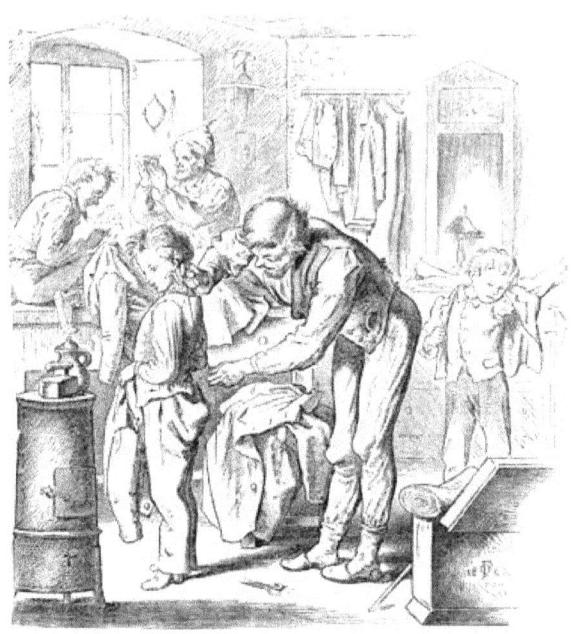

THE NEW JACKET.

This is a tailor's shop, and Master Albert is being measured for a new jacket. His young brother Robert is to have one too.

THE PET BIRD.

How pleased baby is with the pet bird perched on the back of the chair!

FAST ASLEEP.

THE APPLE CUPBOARD.

The children have just found out where mama keeps her apples.

HALF-HOLIDAY.

It is half-holiday, and, as it is wet, Master Fred is lounging about in-doors.

"DON'T FORGET ME."

Baby is sitting in the out-house eating a piece of bread-and-butter. Bob is putting his paw gently upon him, as much as to say, "Don't forget me, baby, but give me a bit, please."

THE BAKERY.

Mary has come to the baker's to buy a new loaf this morning, and she has peeped into the bakery to see how the men make the bread. She must not stay long though, for they are all waiting at home to have their breakfast.

THE TWO LITTLE SISTERS.

These two little girls are sisters, and they are very fond of one another, as sisters should be.

"WAKE UP, DRIVER."

Little Andrew is out early with his grandfather this morning, to take a long ride to the next town. They are asking the driver of a coach to take them, but he is fast asleep on the box.

COMING OUT OF SCHOOL.

The clock has just struck the hour, and the children are coming out of school. They seem to have forgotten that the snow is on the ground, and that it is very slippery. Three of them have fallen down, but I do not think they have hurt themselves, as they seem very merry.

BABY'S FLOWERS.

HELPING TO COOK.

Little Lucy is helping mama to make the nice jams this morning.

THE SNOW MAN.

The children have made a great snow man, and they are lifting up dolly to look at him.

THE ARTIST.

The artist is sitting on a camp-stool, taking a sketch of the cottages yonder. He has put up his umbrella to shelter himself from the sun. The boys seem greatly interested in his work.

TEASING MAMA.

The children seem very troublesome and noisy this afternoon. It is well for them that mama has much patience, or she would be very angry indeed at their bad behaviour.

THE VISIT TO GRANDMAMA.

The children are come to-day on a visit to grandmama. She is telling them they have grown very much lately. But Miss Pry ought not to open grandmama's drawers.

ASLEEP.

Maria has been sitting on the sofa this evening, looking through some picture books. But it is late, and mama has not yet come home, and she has fallen fast asleep with dolly behind her.

WHAT SHALL I DO NEXT?

It is a wet day, and little Laura cannot go out. So she has been playing indoors, and been amusing herself with her dolls. But it still rains, and she is tired of her dolls, and is asking herself what she shall do next to amuse herself. She must have patience, and papa will be home to tea presently.

THE LITTLE LAMB.

"HOLD IT FAST, PRINCE."

This is Alfred, the hunter's little son, who has dressed himself up in his father's belt and hat. Prince seems to know what Alfred says to him.

THE TINMAN.

The tinman is very busy to-day, with his little hammer, shaping a piece of tin. On the floor around him lie watering-pots, coffee-pots, tin pipes, and a variety of useful articles, all made out of tin.

BLIND-MAN'S-BUFF.

WASHING HANDS.

Mama does not like to see her children dirty, so she is washing their hands, and then they can play about again. Baby is looking at his hands to see if they are dirty, and Alice is examining her doll's hands.

A ROUGH RIDE.

Baby is having a ride this morning on his brother's back. It is a rather rough ride, and shakes him very much when his brother runs. But he likes the fun, and will be sorry when his brother is tired, and puts him down. Carlo is barking beside him with all his might.

MAKING SNOW-BALLS.

It is very cold, and the fields are all covered with snow. The children are on their way to school, but they have laid their books down for a few minutes. The boys are in high glee, for they cannot make snow-balls every day, and there is plenty of snow on the ground just now. I dare say they will be sorry when the snow melts.

THE NEW GAME.

Arthur is a clever lad, as every boy and girl in the village knows. He has just invented a new game, and his playfellows are listening to him while he explains it to them. They are to meet him on the common this afternoon after school, and try if they can play at it.

HALF AFRAID.

GRANDPAPA.

It is grandpapa's birthday, and the children have come to congratulate him.

THE ORGAN MAN.

Here, poor organ man, here is a penny for you, and I will sit down with my dolly, on this log of wood, and listen to your pretty tunes.

DO YOU WANT A CARPENTER?

Little William has dressed himself up as a carpenter, and his sister is pretending to be a fine lady. William is asking her if she wants a carpenter, as he has his tools with him, and will be very glad of a job. Susan is sitting outside pretending to be keeping a coffee-stall.

HOW POLITE!

Richard's little cousin has called in this afternoon, and Richard, who is very kind and polite, is handing her some cake, and asking her to have a slice.

TEASING.

Master Sydney is, I am sorry to tell you, very fond of teasing. This is not a nice habit, for, although it may begin in fun, it often ends in a quarrel. His little sister does not like it, and he has been teasing her so long that she is now crying. If she tells his papa of it he will be very angry, as he has often reproved Sydney for this bad habit before, and I was hoping he had broken it off. Sydney ought to do all he can to please his little sister, rather than thus take delight in vexing and annoying her.

BABY'S BATH.

Baby is sitting in his little bathing tub, waiting for his sister to come up and wash him. He is beginning to like the water now, and is quite pleased to sit in it and be washed. At first he did not like it at all, and began to scream at the sight of the tub, but he has now more confidence, and likes it very much. It is nice to have a good wash, especially in hot weather, and all children should early be taught to like cleanliness.

BABY AND RATTLE.

Baby is highly amused to hear his rattle making a noise. The dog seems amused too, for he is jumping up to see what it is all about.

VERY HAPPY.

WAYSIDE FLOWERS.

It is a pity there is not more interest taken in wayside and field flowers, some of which are so very beautiful.

THE CONFECTIONER'S.

This is the shop of Mr. Sweet, the pastrycook. The children have just bought some sweets, and his lad is taking out a large cake on a tray.

OUT IN THE GARDEN.

It is half-holiday to-day, but it is too warm to run about the fields. So Susan and Emma are sitting in the wheelbarrow, at the kitchen door, and enjoying themselves as much as if they were sitting in a fine arbour. They have got puss with them, who seems to like it as much as they do. When the sun sets they will water their flowers, for they have got a nice flower-bed of their own, and some of the flowers are just beginning to blossom.

BEING WASHED.

Baby brother is being washed this morning. He does not sit so quiet as he ought to do, and so his sister has, quite by accident, put the sponge in his eye. No wonder he should be making a wry face over it, and crying. If he had been still this would probably not have happened, as his sister is very careful not to hurt him. I hope the next time he is washed he will try to keep himself quiet.

ONLY A TOADSTOOL.

The children are out early this morning in the wood, to gather mushrooms, and have brought a basket to put them in. They have just found something among the roots of this old tree, which they thought at first was a mushroom, but I fear it is only a toadstool, it looks so very strange.

WATCHING THE MOON.

It is time to put baby to bed, but her sister is showing her the moon, shining out so brightly to-night in the deep blue sky. Baby is looking up at it, and is perhaps wondering what it is up there in the sky, so bright and round. It will shine into her little bed-room nearly all the night long.

FIRST STEPS.

Baby is learning to walk, and is stepping out boldly. Puss looks on quietly, but Tiny is barking with joy.

THE DUCKLINGS.

SUSAN'S SHOP.

Susan is playing at shop, and has placed herself behind a large chair, and is looking out for customers. She has dressed baby up in cook's great bonnet and jacket, and she is supposed to be the customer. And Susan is asking her what she will buy, as her scales are all ready to weigh up anything she wants. Baby is asking her if she sells barley-sugar, as, if she does, she would like to have some.

IN THE NURSERY.

The two little sisters are having fine fun in the nursery this morning. Baby dolly is to have a bath presently. The other dolls have at last got dressed in their new clothes, that have been so long making, and they are being jumped about and walked along as if they were really alive. The children are so fond of their dolls, they seem never tired of playing with them.

SUNDAY MORNING.

It is Sunday morning, and everything is quiet in the village. The blacksmith's hammer is still, the horses are in the stable, and the plough lies in the corner of the field. The children are hastening to the Sunday-school, with their Bible and hymn-book under their arm. Walter Rose is reading a Psalm to his wife and children, and then they will get ready for church.

GIVING DOGGIE A RIDE.

The little sisters have been giving dolly a ride in their basket-chaise. And now they think it is doggie's turn, and they are putting him in the chaise for a ride too. I am afraid he will not sit very nicely, but will be a troublesome rider. Poor dolly is lying on the floor, on her back. I hope she is not hurt.

THE GENTLE COW.

The cow is a quiet creature, and is one of the most useful of all animals. We have to thank the cow for our nice milk, and fresh butter. Mary often carries baby to the window of the cow-shed, and baby takes hold of the cow's horn, it is so harmless and gentle.

THE BOOKBINDER'S.

The children have called in to see the bookbinder's shop, and are looking at a map, which he has varnished for them. Arthur is telling his little sister he thinks he should like to be a bookbinder, it seems such a nice business.

HOW DARK IT IS!

Mama is going to put baby to bed, but she is taking her first to the window to show her how dark it is. And now baby must go to bed, for it is late. The little birds are already asleep beneath the roof, for they go to rest early at night, and rise very early in the morning. It is not so dark as this every night, but to-night the moon is not visible.

PLAYING AT SEE-SAW.

A RIDE DOWN-HILL.

Master Clarence is giving his sister Kate a ride in a wheelbarrow, but, as they are going down-hill, I am afraid she will not have a very comfortable ride, and will be very much jolted. And the next time he takes her out for a ride I hope he will find her something larger and pleasanter to ride in. I dare say she will be very glad to get out and walk presently.

THE THIEF ASLEEP.

Giles Scroggs is a lumpish farmer's boy, fat, silly, and lazy. He has but a faint idea of the use of a book, but he understands well the worth of an apple-dumpling. One morning the sly rogue got up very early to steal some apples, but climbing the wall to return he fell asleep on the top, with three rosy apples at his side, just as our artist has drawn him.

BREAKFAST TIME.

It is breakfast time, and this is a family just seated round the table. One of the little boys has put his plate upon his head, I suppose to attract attention to his wants. Baby stands on mama's knee, and seems determined he will not be forgotten. Papa will have enough to do to cut bread-and-butter for them all.

THE HARVEST FIELD.

It is very hot in the open fields to-day, and the reapers are weary. So they are sitting in the shadow of the sheaves, and are drinking some water, as working in the heat has made them very thirsty. The sun will go down presently, and then it will be cool and pleasant for them to walk home over the fields.

TAKING A WALK.

It is a pleasant spring morning, and the children are out early, taking a walk with mama. She is carrying the baby, and little Alice is taking her new doll by the hand to try and teach her to walk. Albert is riding his wooden horse, and Rover is barking at him, he is so pleased. They are not going far, and will turn back to breakfast presently.

WIND AND RAIN.

How it rains! I am afraid our party in the picture will all be wet to the skin. It is a pity they have only one umbrella among them, and they have a long distance to go before they reach home. It was fine when they started, so they were not prepared for such a storm. But perhaps it will soon be fine again.

WATCHING THE GARDENER.

Gardening is a nice employment, and so little Maria thinks, as with folded arms she watches the gardener attending to his plants. She is thinking how she should like to be putting plants into pots, watching for the seeds to come up, and the buds to expand into blossoms.

ELLEN'S NEW BIBLE.

NOT HURT, I HOPE.

The road is so slippery this morning, after the frost, that little Harriet has just had a fall.

THE SICK BOY.

Master Thomas is very unwell to-day, so he has to stay at home and take some physic.

UNDER THE UMBRELLA.

Ellen and Maria are enjoying themselves in-doors this afternoon. They are sitting on the floor in the nursery, and have put up cook's old market umbrella to cover them. It is so large it makes quite a tent for them to sit under. They have two apples beside them, so I suppose they will have a feast presently.

THE MEETING.

Susan has long been expecting her little cousin from the country, and she has just arrived. When Susan has done kissing her, she will tell her how glad she is to see her, and show her her pretty doll and her playthings. The dog too is jumping up at her and barking, as though he would give her a welcome also.

MEDICINE FOR THE BABY.

James has come to the chemist's shop this morning for medicine for the baby, who is sick.

THE BROKEN CRADLE.

Harriet has just brought her doll's cradle to the carpenter, to get it mended. He is telling her to leave it, and he will soon repair it.

MORE KISSING.

Mama and baby are always kissing one another, and there will be kissing again when papa comes home.

PLAYING AT BOWLS.

THE STROLLING FIDDLER.

Poor old man! He is playing away merrily, though I dare say he is tired, and has perhaps walked many a mile this hot day. If he does not play very well, his music pleases the baby at the window. Here, poor man, is a penny for you.

THE DUNCE.

I am sorry to see that boy with the dunce's cap standing there in the middle of the school. I should think he must feel very much ashamed to be the laughing-stock of his schoolfellows. I do hope he will pay more attention.

THE WINDMILL.

The sails go round, and the corn is ground.

MAKING JAM.

Mama has been boiling some fruit to make jam for the winter, and given the children a large pan which has been used to make it. They are busy getting out every morsel of the syrup, for it is so nice and sweet.

OUR SHOP.

The tailor's children are having some fun, and, with the help of an old chair and their father's sleeve-board, have made themselves a shop.

EXCHANGING DOLLS.

The two cousins are each of them tired of their own doll, and are wanting to exchange. But they do not seem to like to trust one another, and so each is holding out her hand to the other, and neither of them seems willing to give her doll first. Even the dog looks as if he was surprised at them.

LION'S KENNEL.

Robert is cleaning out Lion's kennel this afternoon, for he is very fond of his dog. Lion seems to know well what Robert is doing for him.

LEARNING THE LESSONS.

George and Ellen are both fond of learning, and never neglect their lessons for anything. They learned them perfectly last night, and this morning they are looking them over again before going to school. I have no fear that either George or Ellen will grow up to be dunces.

WHO'LL HAVE THE APPLE?

Reuben is a clever little boy, and for his age knows very much. He has mounted a tree-stump in the garden, and is asking his brothers and sisters some questions. Whoever gives him the best answers is to have that nice apple he is holding up. They all seem puzzled, even the dog and cat.

THE REVERIE.

Little Martha has just come up into her bed-room, and is leaning her head against the chair, thinking of her dream last night. She dreamed that her uncle had invited her to pay him a visit, and she is just now wondering whether her dream will come true, as she likes going there.

KING OF THE CASTLE.

Tom has fastened the gate, and is laughing at his little playfellows, because they cannot get over the palings to him.

THE STEW PAN.

Mama has just gone out of the kitchen, and Miss Pry is looking to see what is in the stew-pan. This is very naughty.

OUR HALF-HOLIDAY.

This is half-holiday, and the four children are going to have a merry game in the fields. Even baby sister is going with her little dolly, and doggie seems determined he will not be left behind. I hope they will spend a pleasant afternoon, and not get into any mischief.

ON THE WALL.

What a daring little boy that young Edward is! He has climbed to the top of the wall, and his young cousins are cheering him. I hope he will not fall, and hurt himself.

"SHALL WE RING THE BELL?"

Poor little boys, they have no one to care for them, for their father and mother are drunken and idle, and send them about to beg. The children have been told that a kind Christian man lives at this house, and they are going to pull the bell and ask him to help them.

BRUSHING SISTER'S HAIR.

Little Emmeline has just been washed and dressed by her mama. So now she has got the hair-brush, and is standing on a chair brushing her sister Caroline's hair. Caroline has very long hair, so I hope Emmeline will not break it, for of course she does not quite understand how to handle the brush.

BABY BROTHER.

Baby brother is a great pet, I can tell you. Mama is afraid to lose sight of him, for fear any accident should happen to him. Jane and Robert watch for his waking up, so eager are they to nurse him, and even doggie jumps up as if he would say "Can I do anything for you?"

OUT IN THE GARDEN.

Julia is playing with her young brother in the garden. The little bird perched up there is looking as if he would like to play with them too. He has a nest in the trees behind, but I dare say he thinks the children are too kind and gentle to molest his pretty little family.

FEEDING THE RABBITS.

The children are busy in the yard this morning feeding the rabbits. They have opened the rabbit-hutch, and are going to give the rabbits some fresh vegetables. The cat behind is looking slyly on, as though she would like to pounce down among them.

AS MAMA DOES.

Little Bertha is having a tea party. The children have been playing, and now they are having tea, and Bertha is pouring it out for them. Even dolly is seated at the table, but they have forgotten to take her bonnet off. When tea is over they will go out and play in the garden.

OFFENDED.

Something has offended master Joseph, and he is leaning there in a sullen mood, and refuses to play any more. His little sisters are coaxing him to play with them again, and one of them in fun has taken his hat off his head. I hope he will not continue to be angry and sullen, for I am sure they did not mean to offend him.

JUST LIKE GRANDPAPA.

Master Samuel is full of fun, and having found his grandpapa's red cap and spectacles, has seated himself very gravely on one of the kitchen chairs, and is pretending to be grandpapa. I hope he will grow up to be as good a man as his grandpapa is. I can wish nothing better for him, I am quite sure.

OFF TO SCHOOL.

The clock has just struck, and Amy, with her school satchel behind her, is just bidding good-bye to her little sister. She wanted to tell her how to dry her doll's clothes, but she cannot stay now.

FLOATING THE DUCKS.

Baby is highly amused this evening. Papa has brought him home two little toy ducks, and mama has put them in some water in a large tub, where they are floating about.

ALBERT'S HORSE.

Albert is fond of striding a wooden horse, with a horn at his side.

WAITING FOR THE RAIN.

The children were just starting for school, when the rain suddenly came on, and prevented them. But it will be over presently.

BREAKFAST FOR MAMA.

Mama is not well this morning, for she took cold yesterday going over the wet fields to visit the poor man who is dying. So she is not up so early as usual, and Harriet is taking her a cup of hot coffee. Harriet will not let the servant wait on her mama when she is ill, because she can herself pay her more attention. She is walking on tip-toe to avoid making a noise, as sick persons like to be quiet.

"MAMA, I DO LOVE YOU SO."

Ethel is a loving little girl, and is always clinging about her mama. Mama wishes to do some knitting just now, but Ethel is clinging to her, and is saying, "Mama, I do love you so." I am afraid mama will not be able to do much knitting while Ethel interrupts her in this manner.

MAKING A PUDDING.

Mama is busy this morning making a pudding, and the children are watching the process with great interest. Richard is asking her whether she is going to use all that great loaf of lump sugar in making it. Tom seems to know better, and is telling him if she were to put all that in the pudding it would be so sweet that they would not like to eat it.

"HOW DO YOU DO, POLL?"

"Poll" is a fine parrot, and seems very happy and contented, swinging there on his perch. He likes to be talked to, and can answer very plain. If you say to him, "How do you do, Poll?" he will answer you, "Quite well, thank you, and how are you?" Poll is quite a companion, he is so intelligent.

JOHN'S NEW TOY.

John is in high glee, for his aunt has bought him a new toy. It is a figure made of paste-board, and it throws out its legs and arms.

THE SECRET.

Emma seems whispering something in her sister's ear as if it was a secret. I do not know why she should whisper, for no one seems near to overhear them. I suppose it is something about their dolls, else about little Fan, who is lying beside them on the floor, and who seems to be very tired.

ELLEN'S DREAM.

Ellen is very fond of animals, and likes to read about them. Papa has just bought her a pretty book, in which she has been reading a good deal about sheep and shepherds. I suppose it is owing to this that she dreamed last night she was a shepherdess, with a crook in her hand, and her sheep lying in the fields around her, just as our artist has drawn in the picture.

QUARRELLING.

This is a sad scene. The two little sisters are quarrelling over their playthings, and I am afraid the dolls will get damaged in their angry strife. The little lamb lies upset on the chair, the little dolly is sprawling on the floor, and the dress of the bigger one will certainly be torn. It is a pity the two sisters should quarrel in this manner, and about such trifles too.

DILIGENT CHARLES.

Charles is one of the most diligent boys in his school. He does not dislike a good game in the playground, but, when you see him there, you may be sure his lessons have all been learned first. The diligent schoolboy generally becomes a successful man, but a dunce seldom gets on in after-life.

TIRED OF IT.

Arthur Jones has been writing some exercises in grammar this morning. He has not done much, but he is quite tired of it already. He wishes the clock would strike twelve, that he might leave off, and spin the top at his side. Shame on you, lazy Arthur!

THE SULKY GIRL.

Here is a little party of children, playing in the wood-yard this afternoon. They have been having some merry games, and had just arranged to meet again next half-holiday. Suddenly one of the little girls took offence at something, and walked away, and would not play any more. It is a pity she is sulky, and so apt to take offence. I dare say her little friends did not intend to offend her.

THE SICK DOLLS.

The two little sisters are making a great fuss just now about their sick dolls. They have been making something warm for them, and are now about to put them to bed in the cradle. One of them is being hushed to sleep. They are taking pains to have the mattress smooth and well shaken up, so that the dolls may have a soft bed. But I am afraid the cradle is not quite big enough for both of them, and if so they will not be very comfortable.

"WHAT SHALL WE DO?"

The poor children have just accidentally broken their pitcher. No wonder they are so sad.

AN AFTERNOON NAP.

Lucy has just been asleep in the great arm-chair. She little thinks what pussy is about.

THE PUMP.

The children are up early this morning getting some water at the pump. The geese are watching them, as if they were longing to have a little of it. Perhaps the little girl will give them some when she has filled her jar, for she is very thoughtful for dumb animals, and they all like her very much, and follow her about. It is a good sign when children are kind to animals.

THE PLAYTHINGS.

Little Ellen seems ill at ease just now. She has got a nice doll, a chest of drawers, and a doll's cradle. But she is coveting her little brother's playthings besides, and seems cross because she cannot have his horse and stable, and little cart. This is very wrong. We should be content with what we have, and not covet what belongs to others.

GRANDMAMA.

Mama has brought the children to see grandmama this afternoon. She is so glad to see them. One of them is handing her some tea.

HELPING COOK.

The children are spending an hour in the kitchen with cook. It is fine fun for them.

IN THE SUMMER-HOUSE.

Baby is hugging and kissing his sister in the summer-house. It is a nice cool place to play in.

THE EMPTY POCKET.

The children are buying some fruit at the fruit stall. Poor little Richard and his sister are walking sadly away, for they have no money.

A STRANGE SEAT FOR DOLLY.

Baby has strayed up into a spare room, where papa keeps some of his old books, and she is having rare fun here all by herself. She has brought up her two dolls, one of which she has seated in a basket, and is finding a seat for the other on a great old clasped book. Papa little thinks what baby is about, but I dare say she will be missed presently, and then they will find her very busy up here.

STUDIOUS HERBERT.

Herbert is a studious boy, fond of books, and is very careful to learn his lessons well. These long winter evenings are very nice for learning, and just now Herbert is making great progress. It is late this evening, but he is not willing to go up to bed till he has learned all his lessons for to-morrow. He would have learned them earlier but he has been to tea with his cousins, and so when he came home just now he lit the lamp, and sat down to his work. When Herbert leaves school I dare say he will get a good situation, as any one will be glad to employ him.

WAITING.

Maria is waiting for her little cousin to come and play with her in papa's bedroom. She is standing on the top of the stairs listening, and is wondering why she does not come. She will come up presently, I suppose, and then they will have a nice game all to themselves, without disturbing any one in the house.

"YOU SHAN'T COME IN."

The boys are at home just now for their holidays, and mama is half distracted with their noise. When it is fine they prefer to be in the fields, but when it is wet they are chasing one another about all the day long. One of them has just run up into this room, and is telling his brothers outside they shall not come in.

CAUGHT.

Master Andrew has just been caught by the old gentleman, who is giving him a few smart strokes with his cane. I am glad of it, for he is a mischievous lad. He was sent to school just now, but instead of hastening there he thought he would stroll through the plantation and see if he could find any birds' nests. Now the old gentleman is very fond of his birds, and will not have them molested. Hearing the crashing of the boughs, he soon discovered the offender, and after a short chase caught him. This beating serves Andrew right, and I hope he will in future leave the poor birds alone.

"BE A GOOD DOLLY."

Louisa is so fond of her dolls. She has two of them, and places a pillow in her little basket chaise, and draws them about the garden. She is as attentive to them as if they were two little babies, and takes more care of them than some thoughtless mothers do of their children. She is going to take them out for a ride this morning, and is kissing them. I hope she will make them a comfortable seat on the pillows, or else they will not have a very nice ride.

THE LITTLE SQUIRREL.

The children are offering some bread to a pretty squirrel their father found in the wood.

NEARLY DRESSED.

Matilda is nearly dressed. She will be ready for her breakfast now in a few minutes, and then must make haste to school.

THE KITES.

There is a nice breeze this afternoon, and this hill-side is just the place for flying a kite. Two kites are already flying merrily up in the sky, and our two young friends will fly theirs when they get a little higher up, near the windmill.

THE PETS.

THE BOOKSELLER.

The boys like to call on Mr. Leaf, because he has such nice books. But sometimes they merely sit down and read them.

TAKING A PHOTOGRAPH.

The squire has called at the studio to-day to have his carte taken, and the photographer is placing him in the best position.

RATHER TIGHT.

Richard has come for a pair of boots, and is trying a pair on, but he thinks they are rather too small for him.

"A LETTER, SIR."

A messenger has just brought the student a letter. The dog is looking at the man rather suspiciously.

MUSING.

Little Hester is leaning on the palings this afternoon, with her head on her hand, as if in a deep study. I wonder what she is musing about. I dare say if the little bird above her could speak he would ask her the subject of her thoughts. I hope they are good, hopeful, cheerful thoughts, and I think they are, judging from her serene and happy countenance.

THE WINGED LETTER-CARRIER.

The pigeon is a pretty creature, and is sometimes useful in carrying letters very long distances. Little Susan is quite overjoyed this morning to find one of papa's pigeons dropping at her feet a letter which it must have carried very many weary miles.

WATCHING PUSSY.

Pussy is very sly in her movements, and little John is watching from the window, to see whether she is up to any mischief. The dog seems, from his look, as if he half suspected her also. The little birds on the bough just above her had better take care of themselves, for Pussy would soon be after them if she once saw them. But she is not likely to catch them, for Pussy has no wings to follow them when they fly away.

THE SLEDGE.

It is a cold winter morning, and the children are amusing themselves by riding in a sledge over the frozen snow. The birds are huddling together on the bare branches, as if they felt the cold very keenly. It is pleasant, no doubt, for the riders, but whether it is for our little friend who is drawing the sledge, I am not sure. At all events, it will warm him this cold morning, and that will no doubt do him good.

A, B, C.

A, B, C, are, as you know, the first three letters of the alphabet, and the children in the picture are just beginning to learn them. It seems hard to them at first, but it will be easy presently. They will soon learn the name and shape of all the letters, and then will go on to learn what letters make a word, and then what meaning the word has. Thus they will soon be able to read and spell every word, and sit down and read the nice books in papa's library.

LITTLE ALFRED'S PRAYER.

My heavenly Father, I thank Thee for all Thy care and kindness, for all Thy mercy and love. I thank Thee for my home and friends, for my comforts and blessings. I commit myself to Thy continued care and kind keeping. I pray that Thou wilt keep all evil from me. And bless my dear friends, and all who are about me. Help me to be sorry for my sins, to please Thee in all things, and to grow in all virtue and godliness. Hear me, my Father, for my dear Saviour's sake. Amen.

"WHICH IS THE WAY, PLEASE?"

Edwin has had a long walk in the country, but in returning home has wandered out of the way, and lost himself. He is just now standing on an eminence in the road, and, seeing some travellers, is shouting to them, and asking them to direct him.

"CAN'T GO OUT YET."

It is pouring heavily, though the boy with the basket does not seem to mind it. Annie is impatient, but she must wait till the rain is over.

THE SCHOOLMASTER.

The old schoolmaster is busy with his pupils this afternoon, and is reading something which they are writing out. Some of the words puzzle little Joseph, and he does not know how to spell them. His tiny brother, who sits at his side, is making straight strokes.

THE SAW-PIT.

It is dinner-time, and the children have just brought their father's dinner to the saw-pit, and are spreading a clean cloth for him on a large log of wood.

THE SLEDGE-CHAIR.

Harriet is giving her little sister a ride in a sledge-chair, and she has got her mama's muff to put her hands in. The rude schoolboys are stopping to quiz the funny chair, but Harriet does not mind their laugh, for she knows her little sister will like the ride.

OFF TO SEA.

Sidney has just bidden his friends good-bye, and is off for his first voyage. He is so fond of the sea that nothing else would please him. His ship is lying out there in the distance, and he is just going on board, as the vessel sails tomorrow for China.

"WANT ANYTHING TO-DAY?"

The poor old man is hobbling along from door to door, to see if he can sell anything.

DON'T BE AFRAID.

Amy has got a penny for the lad who has swept the path, but she is quite afraid of him.

SHOWING BABY THE PICTURES.

Mama is always ready to please her little baby girl in any way she can. She has just got a nice picture-book, and is going to show baby the pictures. Baby is so eager to see them that she has thrown aside her little mug, and trumpet, and woolly lamb, in order to look at them. How pleased she will be for mama to take her on her knee, and explain them to her!

"RATHER FEVERISH."

Master Edmund is lying on the sofa this morning unwell. They have sent for the doctor, who is feeling his pulse, and looking at his tongue. The doctor will send him some medicine presently, but he does not know that it is all through eating too much of that currant tart yesterday.

RINGING THE BELL.

Little May is but a dot of a child to walk down the street all by herself, and ring the school bell. But she can do this quite safely, and does it nearly every day. The bell is rather high up for her to reach it, but she can just stretch her little fat fingers up to it, and pull it, and then some one opens the door for her. She is very fond of going to school, and always contrives to be there early.

SCHOOL OVER.

The clock has just struck, and the children are coming down-stairs to go home. They are glad to go, the more so as it is half-holiday to-day, and as it is fine weather they want to be at their games in the fields. The little girl coming down the stone stairs is leaning over the rails looking for her brother, who is just below and does not see her. He will wait for her, I am sure, for he would not be so unkind as to go home without her, for he is very fond of his little sister.

THE BOOT CUPBOARD.

This is our boot cupboard, where we keep the blacking and brushes, and papa's boot-jack. I will tell you whom they belong to, all these five pairs. The tall big ones belong to dear papa, as you may suppose, and are strong ones, as he has to walk very much. Mama's boots are not kept here, but in her own bed-room. Then the next tall pair belong to brother Richard, and are almost as large as papa's. The pair between Richard's boots belong to sister Mary; and the pair nearer the door, to little Susan. The tiny pair next the door, are dear little baby's, but they are not of much use to him, for his fat little feet need a larger pair.

Milton Keynes UK
Ingram Content Group UK Ltd.
UKHW031031210324
439796UK00008B/690